# UNDER THE SEA FIELD GUIDE

## Activities, Doodling, and Fun Facts

Written by Cynthia Stierle

Silver Dolphin

San Diego, California

# Counting at School

When fish swim together in the same area, it's called a shoal. When they are moving together in the same direction at the same time, it's called a school. How many fish can you count in this scene? (Answer on page 22.)

# Coral Maze

Help this little fish find its way through the coral maze.
(Answer on page 22.)

**Start**

**Finish**

# Whe.e Are the Fis..?

Coral reefs are busy places. Use your stickers to add fish to the scene.

# Crossword

Dive right into this crossword puzzle. Look at the pictures and fill in the numbered boxes with the name of the animal that you see. We've done one for you. (Answers on page 22.)

**Across**

3

4

6

7

8

**Down**

1

2

3

5

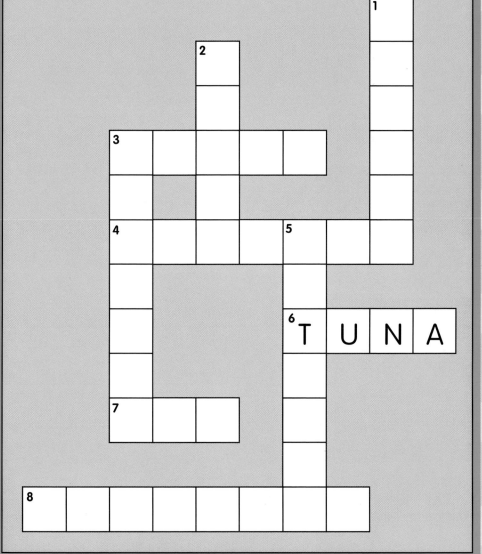

RAY     SHARK     WHALE

SEA HORSE     SEA STAR     TURTLE

OCTOPUS     ANEMONE     TUNA

# Help the Kelp

Sea otters help the kelp by eating sea urchins. Can you help the sea otter by finding the shortest path to the bottom?

(Answer on page 22.)

**Path 1 Start**  **Path 2 Start**  **Path 3 Start**

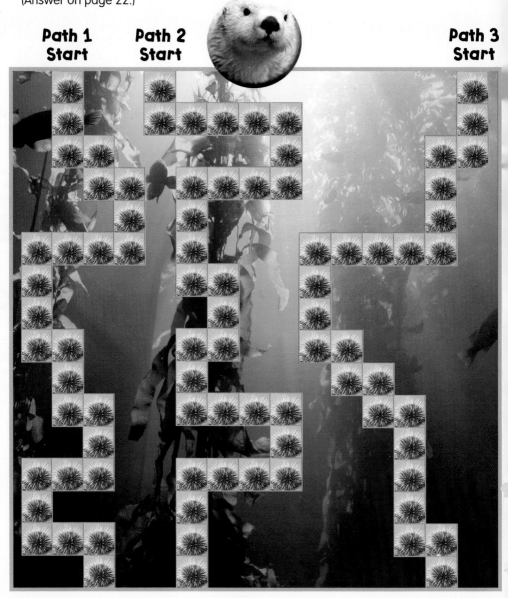

**Path 1 =** ____    **Path 2 =** ____    **Path 3 =** ____

# Click!

When you go on an undersea adventure, you'll want to keep a record of your journey by taking pictures and notes. You've just snapped a picture of an awesome animal.

Draw your animal in the camera lens.

Now add some notes about what you saw.

# Shark Search

Try to find the different shark names hidden in the grid below. The names are listed on the opposite page. Look across, down, and diagonally to find them. (Answers on page 22.)

| G | T | T | V | I | N | G | U | S | L | H | W | F |
|---|---|---|---|---|---|---|---|---|---|---|---|---|
| G | R | D | O | T | S | B | B | M | K | A | N | A |
| L | R | E | W | H | A | L | E | A | N | M | Q | F |
| E | L | L | A | W | D | U | S | S | Y | M | E | C |
| O | O | T | W | T | I | E | X | O | X | E | P | A |
| P | Q | E | H | D | W | X | V | Q | R | R | S | R |
| A | S | I | J | H | I | H | P | P | M | H | F | I |
| R | Z | E | B | R | A | V | I | C | X | E | Z | B |
| D | U | B | J | K | X | T | F | T | A | A | A | B |
| B | S | B | L | B | K | I | W | U | E | D | U | E |
| B | B | U | E | C | J | G | C | R | S | M | O | A |
| U | U | Q | A | U | V | E | N | W | P | B | O | N |
| L | F | L | Q | V | H | R | U | Z | A | T | T | R |
| L | B | X | R | M | M | F | R | X | A | J | J | E |
| C | O | S | B | I | E | C | S | T | T | E | R | E |
| G | V | L | E | M | O | N | E | T | M | S | V | F |

CARIBBEAN REEF

NURSE

WHALE

HAMMERHEAD

BULL

BLACKTIP REEF

GREAT WHITE

LEOPARD

BLUE

TIGER

LEMON

ZEBRA

# Find That Fish

Many coral reef fish have thin, flat shapes that allow them to swim easily through the reef. These fish look different when you see them in color.

1

2

3

4

5

6

A_____

B_____

C_____

D_____

E_____

F_____

But could you tell them apart if you could see only their shadows? Match each shadow below to the fish in the picture by writing the correct number next to each shadow.

(Answers on page 22.)

G_____

H_____

I_____

J_____

K_____

L_____

# What's Different?

There are six differences between these two photos. Can you find them all?

(Answers on page 22.)

# A Closer Look

Someone took pictures of dolphins and whales, but the camera was too close. Try to match the close-ups to the correct animals. (Answers on page 22.)

A_____    B_____    C_____

D_____    E_____    F_____

19

# For the Scrapbook

Keep a record of your explorations. On the left side of the scrapbook, draw a picture of your favorite marine animal.

Now imagine that you have just discovered a new sea creature. What does it look like and what would you call it? Draw the picture and write its name on the right side of the book.

# Answers

**PAGE 4:** 20 fish

**PAGE 5:**

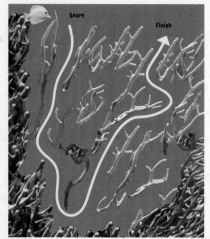

**PAGE 12:**

| | | | | | | | | | | | |
|---|---|---|---|---|---|---|---|---|---|---|---|
| G | T | T | V | I | N | G | U | S | L | H | W | F |
| G | R | D | O | T | S | B | B | M | K | A | N | A |
| L | R | E | W | H | A | L | E | A | N | M | Q | F |
| E | L | L | A | W | D | U | S | S | Y | M | E | C |
| O | O | T | W | T | I | E | X | O | X | E | P | A |
| P | Q | E | H | D | W | X | V | Q | R | R | R | R |
| A | S | I | J | H | I | H | P | P | M | H | F | I |
| R | Z | E | B | R | A | V | I | C | X | E | Z | B |
| D | U | B | J | K | X | T | F | T | A | A | A | B |
| B | S | B | L | B | K | I | W | U | E | D | U | E |
| B | B | U | E | C | J | G | C | R | S | M | O | A |
| U | U | Q | A | U | V | E | N | W | P | B | O | N |
| L | F | L | Q | V | H | R | U | Z | A | T | T | R |
| L | B | X | R | M | M | F | R | X | A | J | J | E |
| C | O | S | B | I | E | C | S | T | T | E | R | E |
| G | V | L | E | M | O | N | E | T | M | S | V | F |

**PAGES 8-9:**

**PAGES 14-15:** A10, B3, C7, D12, E1, F11, G4, H2, I6, J8, K9, L5

**PAGES 16-17:**

**PAGES 10-11:** Path 3 is the shortest. (Path 1=27; Path 2=31; Path 3=25)

**PAGES 18-19:** A5, B6, C3, D1, E4, F2